FAT BOMBS

SWEET & SAVORY SNACKS FOR THE KETOGENIC DIET, PALEO DIET & LOW-CARB DIET

ANDREA J. CLARK

CONTENTS

INTRODUCTION

The Ketogenic Diet is a fantastic solution to maintaining a healthy diet and healthy weight. It is known to lower your blood sugar and bad cholesterol. However, if you're following a Ketogenic diet or have done it before, you definitely know that feeling of wanting to give yourself a special treat from time to time. I totally get it. And that's when these delicious fat bombs come in.

WHAT ARE FAT BOMBS

Fat bombs are savory or sweet treats made from a combination of ingredients, including, but not limited to: nuts, seeds, butter, and coconut oil. They were especially designed for people following the Ketogenic diet and LCHF diet, but they fit other low carb diets that induce ketosis as well.

While the name "fat bomb" might sound scary, fat bombs are an excellent way to get a concentrated source of healthy fats that will provide energy and even satisfy your sweet tooth. In this cookbook, you will find 30 delicious and easy-to-make fat bombs recipes that will support you along your Ketogenic or low carb journey.

WHEN TO EAT THEM

Fat bombs can be uses as a quick breakfast, quick snack in the mid-afternoon, or before or after a workout. They'll give you extra fuel during your day, and they'll certainly give you the fuel you need to work out to lose the weight you want. Of course, if you're just using them to maintain your diet, then using them as a breakfast or snack is usually best.

HOW TO USE THIS BOOK

The book contains 15 sweet fat bombs and 15 savory fat bombs. Every recipe clearly indicates the prep time, total time, servings as well as nutritional facts per serving. There are also labels for each recipe such as nut free, dairy free, and no sweetener for those of you who are allergic to certain types of food. Read through the following two chapters to understand the basic ingredients and tools you will need for making these fat bomb recipes, and you are good to go.

Below you'll find a recipe that's used as a sample. It's also your first bonus recipe that you'll find in this book.

SAMPLE RECIPE: MAPLE NUT FUDGE

This maple fudge is a great keto bomb, and you'll find that it tastes sweet and delicious without any need for granulated sugar.

- Prep Time: 10 Minutes
- Total Time: 25-35 Minutes
- Serves: 24

Ingredients:

- ¼ Cup Grass-Fed Butter
- ½ Cup Almond Butter
- 8 Ounces Cream Cheese
- ¼ Cup Swerve Sweetener
- 1 Teaspoon Maple Extract

Directions:

1. Take a small saucepan and melt your butter and almond butter over medium-high heat.
2. Next, add your swerve until it dissolves. The mixture should begin to bubble slightly. Add in maple extract and cream cheese.
3. Use a hand mixer, mix until combined.
4. Take an 8x8 oven-safe pan, and line it with parchment paper. Pour your mixture into the pan, and then refrigerate overnight. Cut into 24 one-inch cubes to serve.

Recipe Tips:

You can place your mixture into the blender, blending until combined so that you won't have to whip it later. It simply won't separate.

For added variety, you can add a cup of pecans or walnuts. Just fold them in after blending your mixture.

Nutritional Facts Per Serving:

- Total Carbs: 3.25 grams
- Dietary Fiber: 0.5 grams
- Net Carbs: 2.75 grams
- Protein: 1.78 gram
- Total Fat: 7.52 grams
- Calories: 85

CHAPTER 1

ESSENTIAL FAT BOMB INGREDIENTS

Almost all fat bomb recipes have to keep chilled so that they harden. Fat bombs melt quickly due to their high-fat content. This is why most fat bombs are done in bite size portions. Fat bombs are meant to be easy to make, so there's no reason to stress about them.

THREE BASIC TYPES OF INGREDIENTS

A Fat Base

Since it's a fat bomb, healthy fat is a necessity. Common fat base includes cream cheese, MCT oil, grass-fed butter, or coconut oil. Coconut oil is considered to be the healthiest oil that can be used in a fat bomb because your body doesn't store these fats. Instead, they're immediately used for energy.

A Flavoring/Sweetener

The most common ones are cocoa powder, flavored

syrups and spices. We will cover the types of sweeteners you can use later.

A Mix-In

This is something you add to add the texture. These often include low carb fruits, shredded coconut, seeds and nuts.

COMMON FAT BOMB INGREDIENTS

In this section, you'll learn a few common ingredients that are used in fat bombs and in the recipes of this book.

Nuts & Seeds:

Almond, walnuts and pecans are the most common nuts to use in fat bomb recipes. Remember to activate them before using them for your fat bomb recipes.

How to Activate Them: You can activate nuts by soaking or sprouting them. This makes them more easily digested, allowing your body to more easily absorb their nutrients. Soaking and drying them can also cause a crunchier texture that has a more potent flavor as well. If you want to soak nuts, it's simple. All you need to do is place them in a bowl and fill it with either water or salted water. Keep it at room temperature overnight. You can then drain them, spreading it out over parchment paper on a baking sheet, placing it in the oven on low heat or a dehydrator for twelve to twenty-four hours. You will need to stir them occasionally to make sure that it's completely dry. Store them in an airtight container after they are done.

For almonds and hazelnuts, the soaking time is 8-12 hours

and the dehydrating temperature is 120 -150 degrees F (49-65 degrees C).

For pine nuts, walnuts, pecans, Brazil nuts and Macadamia nuts, the soaking time is 4-8 hours and the dehydrating temperature is 120 -150 degrees F (49-65 degrees C).

For cashews and pistachios, the soaking time is 2-3 hours and the dehydrating temperature is 200 - 250 degrees F (93-121 degrees C)

Butter:

The butter that you need to use is grass-fed and organic.

Coconut Product:

These coconut products are also very common ingredients for fat bombs.

- **Coconut Flour:** It's made from coconut meat and the oil has been removed.

- **Coconut Cream:** Coconut cream or creamed coconut milk can be used because it's high in fat. To cream coconut milk, you need to place the can in the refrigerator, leaving it overnight. Open that can, spooning the solidified coconut milk out, discarding the liquid. Don't shake the can before opening.

- **Coconut Butter:** Coconut butter is made from a coconut that's been dehydrated, and then the process is the same as the nut and seed butters.

- **Coconut Milk:** Coconut milk is a liquid that's extracted from the meat of a coconut that's been grated, and it has as much fat as heavy whipping cream. You can get dehydrated coconut milk powder as well.

- **Desiccated Coconut:** Desiccated coconut is shredded, and it's from the meat of the coconut. You need to get the type that's unsweetened.

- **Coconut Oil:** Coconut oil is easily digested and used immediately as energy.

Cacao & Dark Chocolate:

Cacao and dark chocolate, in general, are a great way to flavor your fat bombs.

- **Cacao Butter:** Cacao butter or cocoa butter can be used, and it's considered to be pure fat. It's made from extracting the cacao beans, which have a high smoke point, long shelf life, and has mostly saturated fats and monounsaturated fatty acids. It stays solid at room temperature.

- **Cacao Powder:** Cacao powder can be used, but it's often referred to as cocoa powder. It's made from the raw cacao mass, but make sure to use a Sweetener Free version because many versions have milk fats, oils or sugars.

- **Cacao Paste:** Cacao paste is also known as cacao liquor or even as unsweetened chocolate, and it becomes a liquid when heated.

- **Cacao Nibs:** Cacao nibs are the beans that have been roasted and separated from the husk. They're then crushed into small pieces, and many people confuse them with dark chocolate chips, but they don't contain sugar.

Full-Fat Dairy:

Cheese and cream cheese are used often. You can also use heavy cream and mascarpone cheese.

Sweeteners:

Of course, you can't just use sugar in a keto fat bomb, but you can use these sweeteners. Some of the best sweeteners are Erythritol, Swerve and Stevia. FDA recognizes these sweeteners as safe, and they won't affect your blood sugar levels. These sweeteners are healthy, and you should not experience any side effects.

Other Ingredients:

- **Low-Carb Fruits:** Not every fruit is something that you can use for fat bomb recipes, but berries and cherries are. You can also use watermelon, cantaloupe, honeydew and even peaches.

- **Raw Eggs:** There are some recipes that may call for raw eggs, but if you're worried about any potential risk of salmonella, you will want to use pasteurized eggs to be safer. If you want to pasteurize your eggs at home, put the eggs in a saucepan and cover them with water. Heat it to around 140 degrees F, and then allow them to stay in the water for three minutes. This will kill off any potential bacteria, and then you can refrigerate them. The eggs will be good for six to eight weeks.

- **Vanilla:** If there is a recipe that calls for vanilla, you'll need to use a sugar-free vanilla extract. You can also use natural vanilla powder, which is made from the seeds of the vanilla bean.

CHOOSING GOOD INGREDIENTS

Now that you know the common ingredients you'll find, you need to know how to choose your ingredients. When you're looking for ingredients to make your healthy fat bombs, you need to look for ingredients that have healthy fats. Make sure that they have no or extremely small amount of sugar. Another thing you need to keep in mind that your ingredients should have low carbohydrates.

You should check the net carbs of your ingredients. To calculate net carbs, the following formula is used:

NET CARBS = TOTAL CARBS – DIETARY FIBER

The net carbs are what are important in keeping a healthy diet, because they will show you the amount of carbs that will affect your blood sugar.

CHAPTER 2

PREPARING TO MAKE YOUR FAT BOMBS

When you're ready to make your fat bombs, you'll want to have a clean kitchen and everything prepared. There are some basic tools that you should have in your kitchen when you're preparing to make Ketogenic fat bombs.

TOOLS YOU'LL NEED

Here are the suggested tools that you'll find useful to make fat bombs, but you don't need every single thing. For example, if you have a food processor, then you can leave out the high-powered blender. Just choose what works best for you.

- **Food Processor:** A food processor will usually replace a blender, but you won't get things as smooth as you would with a high-powered blender, which can make it hard to make ice cream recipes or smooth nut butter. However, a food processor will work for the majority of your keto fat bomb recipes, especially the ones that you find in this book. Keep in mind that you'll want one that is easy to take apart and clean.

- **Blender**: If you don't want chunks, you're going to want to get a high-performance blender. Your standard blender just won't cut it, especially if you're trying to make your own nut butter. Of course, there are high-performance blenders in every price range, so make sure that you get the one that's right for you. Keep in mind that you'll want one that is easy to take apart and clean.

- **Ice Cream Maker:** You don't need this if you like chunky ice cream, but if you like soft serve or softer ice cream in general, then this will come in handy for some of the recipes. Though, it's still completely up to you, and you'll later find ways that you can soften your ice cream without an ice cream maker.

- **Basic Silverware:** You'll want to stir with a wooden spoon most of the time, but mashing fruit can be easier with an actual masher or fork. Just make sure that everything is clean and pulled out to save you time.

PREP BEFORE STARTING

You're going to want to prep before starting making your recipe. In other words, you'll need to measure everything in advance. It is actually quicker to do so because you're not worried about ruining your recipe in the meantime, especially if a recipe is time-sensitive. Also, try to group your ingredients and materials together so that you aren't running all over your kitchen to find what you want. Cleaning as you go will also help to make sure that there is less mess if you feel the recipe is complicated. Luckily, most of the recipes in this book are simple enough that you shouldn't need to clean as you go.

HOW TO MAKE NUT BUTTER

Nut butter is often needed in fat bomb recipes, so here are some bonus recipes for you. You're about to learn how to make some basic nut butter so that you don't have to depend on the stores around you to have such an essential ingredient that you'll need.

ALMOND BUTTER

Many people love almond butter. With this homemade recipe, you can still enjoy it while on the keto diet. You'll love this creamy and one ingredient recipe. There's no need to add sugar to make it tasty. You can use a cookie sheet if you don't have a roasting pan. Just remember that the serving size is based off a tablespoon, and the exact amount will depend on how much you blend it. It'll last up to two weeks in the fridge.

- Prep Time: 5 Minutes
- Total Time: 30 Minutes
- Serves: 16
- Sweetener Free, Dairy Free

Ingredients:

- 2 Cups Unsalted Raw Almonds

Directions:

1. Start by preheating your oven to 350 degrees F (180 degrees C), and place your almonds on a roasting sheet, and then proceed to roast for 5 minutes.
2. Let the almonds cool, and then dump them in the food processor. Start to process it, and every 2-3 minutes you'll need to scrape the sides. You will be blending for 13-15 minutes, depending on how smooth you want your almond butter to be.
3. Keep it in the fridge.

Nutritional Facts per serving (1 Tablespoon)

- Carbs: 2.5 grams
- Dietary Fiber: 2 grams
- Net Carbs: 0.5 grams
- Protein: 3.5 grams
- Total Fat: 7.5 grams
- Calories: 80

COCONUT & PECAN BUTTER

Pecan butter is great, but when you mix it with coconut, it has a smooth and light flavor that is sure to go great on its own or any recipe that calls for nut butter. If you want a nut butter that has some kick to it, then this is definitely the recipe for you.

Of course, if you toast your coconut and pecans for a few minutes before pulsing them, then you'll get an even stronger flavor. Remember that you can add cinnamon if you like!

- Prep Time: 5 Minutes
- Cook Time: 20 Minutes
- Serves: 8
- Dairy Free & No Sweetener

Ingredients:

- 2 Cups Unsweetened Shredded Coconut
- 1 Cup Pecan Nuts
- 1 Teaspoon Vanilla Extract
- ½ Teaspoon Cinnamon
- ½ Teaspoon Salt

Directions:

1. Place your pecan nuts and shredded coconut into the food processor, and process it until it's finely chopped.
2. Add your vanilla extract, cinnamon and salt and keep processing it for thirty to sixty seconds. Scrape the sides, and then pulse more. Process until you get the desired consistency, and then store it at room temperature.

Nutritional Values per 2 Tablespoons

- Total Carbs: 6.5 grams
- Dietary Fiber: 4.4 grams
- Net Carbs: 2.1 grams
- Protein: 5 grams
- Total Fat: 11.6 grams
- Calories: 154

BRAZIL NUT & MACADAMIA NUT BUTTER

Like most nut butter, it's going to last longer in the fridge than at room temperature. Of course, you'll find that one benefit of this one is that it has a hint of vanilla, and you don't have to blend nearly as long. In under five minutes, you'll have about 1 ¼ cups of delicious nut butter ready to use in a recipe or eat on your own. Some people like to use a seasoned sea salt like pink Himalayan sea salt to give this recipe a little extra boost.

- Prep Time: 5 Minutes
- Total Time: 5 Minutes
- Serves: 10
- Dairy Free, Sweetener Free

Ingredients:

- 2 Cups Macadamia Nuts
- 8-10 Brazil Nuts
- ½ Teaspoon Vanilla Extract
- ¼ Teaspoon Salt

Directions:

1. Start by placing your Brazil nuts, vanilla, macadamias, and salt in a food processor, and start to blend.
2. Blend until you get your desired consistency. It'll take about two to four minutes depending on how smooth you want it.

You can store at room temperature for about a week, but if you store it in the fridge, you can store it for a month.

Nutrition Facts per Serving (2 tablespoons):

- Total Carbs: 4.3 grams
- Dietary Fiber: 2.7 grams
- Net Carbs: 1.7 grams
- Protein: 2.8 grams
- Total Fat: 23.6 grams
- Calories: 225

CHAPTER 3

15 SWEET FAT BOMB RECIPES

Anyone on a ketogenic diet knows that sugar is a huge no-no, but that doesn't mean that you can't take care of your sweet tooth. What sweetener you will use will mostly depend on your preference, but you'll find that some recipes call for liquid and others call for powder sweetener. Use what you feel is best, and remember that all recipes can be tweaked if you'd like it a little sweeter or a little less sweet.

RAVING RASPBERRY FAT BOMBS

These raspberry fat bombs are sure to help with any sweet tooth, and if you want them to harden quicker you can cool them in the freezer for 15 minutes. There's no reason to wait to try this lovely recipe, and you'll certainly be raving about it to all of your friends. You can use fresh raspberries as well, which is often a little sweeter. If you're using fresh raspberries, you'll need to freeze them for two to three hours.

- Prep Time: 5 Minutes
- Total Time: 25-30 Minutes
- Serves: 12
- Dairy Free, Nut Free

Ingredients:

- ½ Cup Coconut Butter
- ½ Cup Coconut Oil
- ½ Cup Raspberries, Freeze Dried
- ½ Cup Shredded Coconut, Unsweetened
- ¼ Cup Powdered Sugar Substitute (can be Swerve)

Directions:

1. Take your food processor, and pulse your raspberries until they turn into a fine powder.
2. Combine your coconut oil, coconut butter, shredded coconut, and sweetener in a saucepan, cooking over medium heat and stirring until fully melted.
3. Stir in your raspberry powder after you remove it from heat, and then pour it into your molds. 4. Keep it refrigerated until it's solid.

Nutrition Facts per Serving:

- Total Carbs: 3.2 grams
- Dietary Fiber: 0.8 grams
- Net Carbs: 2.5 grams

- Protein: 0.3 grams
- Total Fat: 18 grams
- Calories: 169

COCONUT KETO CANDY

If you love candy and coconut, then you're sure to love this coconut-rich candy. Remember that an ice cube tray will work in a pinch, but you can make it more decorative with silicone molds of your choice. Add a little more sugar substitute if you want it to be a little sweeter. Just remember that you'll need to melt your coconut oil in advance, and virgin coconut oil would be the healthiest choice.

- Prep Time: 5 Minutes
- Total Time: 15 Minutes
- Serves: 10
- Dairy Free, Nut Free

Ingredients:

- ⅓ Cup Coconut Butter, Softened
- ⅓ Cup Coconut Oil, Melted
- 1 Ounce Shredded Coconut, Unsweetened
- 1 Teaspoon Sugar Substitute

Directions:

1. Start by mixing all of your ingredients together, and make sure that the sugar substitute is well dissolved.
2. Pour into silicone molds, and then refrigerate for about an hour.

Nutrition Facts per Serving:

- Total Carbs: 0.8 gram
- Dietary Fiber: 0.2 grams
- Net Carbs: 0.6 grams
- Protein: 0.3 grams
- Total Fat: 11 grams
- Calories: 104

MINTY CHOCOLATE FAT BOMBS

These are multi-layered fat bombs with one amazing layer of pure mint and other layers of a chocolate minty goodness that will melt in your mouth. You can make your own chocolate with cocoa powder and coconut oil, whipping it together. Though, if you have 85% dark chocolate, then that is allowed as well.

- Prep Time: 10 Minutes

- Total Time: 20 Minutes
- Serves: 6
- Dairy Free, Nut Free

Ingredients:

- ½ Cup Coconut Oil, Melted
- 2 Tablespoons Cocoa Powder
- 1 Tablespoon Granulated Stevia (or sweetener of choice)
- ½ Teaspoon Peppermint Essence

Directions:

1. Start by melting your coconut oil, and adding your peppermint essence and sweetener.
2. Add cocoa powder to half of the mixture and mix well in another bowl.
3. Pour the chocolate mixture into the silicone molds, and then place them in the fridge. Refrigerate for 5-10 minutes.
4. Make the mint layer by pouring the mint mixture into the silicon molds. Refrigerate for another 5-10 minutes.
5. Pour the last layer of chocolate mixture into the molds. Refrigerate and let harden.

Nutrition Facts per Serving:

- Total Carbs: 1.15 grams
- Dietary Fiber: 0.7 grams

- Net Carbs: 0.45 grams
- Protein: 0.4 grams
- Total Fat: 18.5 grams
- Calories: 161

STRAWBERRY CHEESECAKE MINIS

Cream cheese is your best friend when it comes to fat bombs, and these strawberry cheesecake minis are no different. They'll make sure that you aren't missing strawberry cheesecake just for choosing a healthier diet. If you want a slightly richer flavor, then add a little more vanilla. Also, if you don't have fresh strawberries on hand, frozen strawberries will work, too. I prefer to keep them frozen, but storing them in your refrigerator will work as well.

- Prep Time: 5 Minutes
- Total Time: 15-20 Minutes
- Serves: 8
- Nut Free

Ingredients:

- ½ Cup Strawberries, Fresh & Mashed
- ¾ Cup Cream Cheese, Softened
- ¼ Cup Coconut Oil, Softened
- 10-15 Drops Liquid Stevia
- 1 Teaspoon Vanilla Extract

Directions:

1. Start by combining all of the ingredients in a bowl, and mixing with a hand mixer until completely smooth. You can also do this in a high-speed blender.
2. Spoon into mini muffin tins, and place in the freezer. It'll take about two hours to set, and then you can place them in the fridge.

Nutritional Facts per Serving

- Total Carbs: 1.55 grams
- Dietary Fiber: 0.2 grams
- Net Carbs: 1.35 grams
- Protein: 1.66 grams
- Total Fat: 13.27 grams
- Calories: 129

LOVELY LEMON BOMBS

These lemon bombs are great for any lemon enthusiast out there. Sweeten them with your keto diet-friendly sweetener to preference. Any coconut oil can be used, but virgin coconut oil will have a lighter taste. Make sure that the lemon extract is either sugar-free or homemade.

- Prep Time: 5-10 Minutes
- Total Time: 35-45 Minutes

- Serves: 16
- Dairy Free, Nut Free

Ingredients:

- ¾ Cup Coconut Butter, Softened
- ¼ Cup Virgin Coconut Oil, Softened
- 2 Tablespoons Lemon Extract
- ¼ Tablespoon Lemon Zest
- 15-20 Drops Stevia Extract

Directions:

1. Start by mixing your coconut butter and coconut oil until blended.
2. Add lemon extract, lemon zest and liquid sweetener and stir. Make sure that it's completely blended.
3. Take mini muffin paper cups, and put a tablespoon of the mixture in each one before placing them in the fridge.
4. Refrigerate them until they're solid. This can take anywhere from thirty minutes to an hour depending on where you place them and what temperature your fridge is set at. Pop one out when you want to eat it.

Nutrition Facts per Serving (1 Mini Muffin Cup)

- Total Carbs: 0.15 grams

- Dietary Fiber: 0.05 grams
- Net Carbs: 0.1 grams
- Protein: 0.01 grams
- Total Fat: 13.6 grams
- Calories: 118

SWEET GINGER BOMBS

This is a great savory recipe if you love ginger. Just get your favorite sweetener, and you'll have these ginger bombs in no time at all. If you don't have silicone molds, then you can simply put them in an ice tray. If you love ginger, don't hesitate to add more!

- Prep Time: 5 Minutes
- Total Time: 20 Minutes
- Serves: 10

- Dairy Free, Nut Free

Ingredients:

- ⅓ Cup Coconut Butter, Softened
- ⅓ Cup Coconut Oil, Softened
- 2 Tablespoons Shredded Coconut, Unsweetened
- 1 Teaspoon Powdered Sweetener
- 1 Teaspoon Ginger Powder

Directions:

1. Mix all of your ingredients, and then pour them into a jug. Make sure that you dissolve the sweetener.
2. Once it's dissolved, pour the mixture in silicon molds, and then refrigerate for at least 10 minutes.

Nutrition Facts per Serving (1 fat bomb)

- Total Carbs: 2.2 grams
- Dietary Fiber: 1.4 grams
- Net Carbs: 0.8 grams
- Protein: 0.5 grams
- Total Fat: 12.8 grams
- Calories: 120

A KETO TAKE ON ALMOND JOY

Yes, you have to get rid of the Almond Joy bars when you're on a keto diet. But this recipe makes a pretty good substitute! It's really easy to make and taste delicious. Just make sure that you have almond butter made already.

- Prep Time: 5 Minutes
- Total Time: 15 Minutes
- Serves: 4
- Dairy Free

Ingredients:

- 2 Tablespoons Almond Butter
- 2 Tablespoons Coconut Oil, Melted
- 2 Tablespoons Cocoa Powder
- 1 Tablespoon Coconut Flour
- 85% Dark Chocolate, Melted
- Splenda to Taste

Directions:

1. Start by mixing your coconut oil and your cocoa powder together, making sure that it's blended well.
2. Add almond butter, mixing until it's completely smooth.
3. Add coconut flour and Splenda. Continue to mix until smooth.
4. Roll into balls and place on parchment paper before freezing. It should take 10 minutes for them to freeze.
5. Dip each ball in the melted dark chocolate to coat.
6. Store them in the fridge.

Nutrition Facts per Serving

- Total Carbs: 6.48 grams
- Dietary Fiber: 2.4 grams
- Net Carbs: 4.08 grams
- Protein: 2.7 grams
- Total Fat: 14.6 grams
- Calories: 157

CHOCOLATE & CAYENNE BOMBS

Nothing goes better than chocolate and cayenne. Depending on how spicy you like them, you can add more or less cayenne pepper.

- Prep Time: 5 Times
- Total Time: 15 Minutes
- Serves: 12

Ingredients:

- ¼ Cup Coconut Oil
- ¼ Cup Salted Butter, Melted
- ¼ Cup Almond Butter
- 2 Tablespoons Cocoa Powder
- 3 Teaspoons Liquid Sweetener
- ¼ Teaspoon Cayenne Pepper

Directions:

1. Melt coconut oil and butter in a saucepan over low heat.
2. Mix all of your ingredients together in a mixing bowl, and then pour them into silicon molds of your choice.
3. Freeze for at least 30 minutes before eating.

Nutrition Facts per Serving

- Total Carbs: 2.85 grams
- Dietary Fiber: 0.8 grams
- Net Carbs: 2.05 grams
- Protein: 1.42 grams
- Total Fat: 10.14 grams
- Calories: 102

ICY MOCHA FAT BOMBS

For all the coffee lovers out there, this mocha recipe will cure that coffee craving! These chilled mocha fat bombs will do the trick for any coffee or chocolate craving.

- Prep Time: 10 Minutes
- Total Time: 1 Hour 10 Minutes
- Serves: 12
- Nut Free

Ingredients:

- 8.5 Ounces Cream Cheese
- 2 Tablespoons Powdered Sweetener
- 2 Tablespoons Cocoa Powder, Unsweetened
- ¼ Cup Strong Coffee, Chilled
- 2.5 Ounces Dark Chocolate, Melted
- 1 Ounce Cocoa Butter, Melted

Directions:

1. Start by adding your coffee, cream cheese, cocoa powder, and sweetener in a blender, and pulse until it's completely smooth.
2. Roll about two tablespoons of the mixture into small bowls, putting them on a baking sheet lined with parchment paper. This recipe should make twelve.
3. Now, blend the melted dark chocolate and cocoa butter until smooth.
4. Roll your balls in the chocolate coating and place them back on the tray.
5. Freeze them for 1 hour or until set.

Nutrition Facts per Serving

- Total Carbs: 6.52 grams
- Dietary Fiber: 0.7 grams
- Net Carbs: 5.82 grams
- Protein: 2.4 grams
- Total Fat: 9.9 grams
- Calories: 120

SWEET VANILLA CHEESECAKE FAT BOMBS

This is another extremely simple and sweet recipe that will give you the fat that you need in a fat bomb. The cream cheese is simply flavored with vanilla, but you'll find that it certainly packs flavor.

- Prep Time: 5 Minutes
- Total Time: 15 Minutes
- Serves: 8
- Nut Free

Ingredients:

- 6 Ounces Cream Cheese, Softened
- ½ Cup Heavy Whipping Cream
- 1 ½ Teaspoons Vanilla Extract
- ¼ Cup Erythritol or Other Sugar Substitute
- ¼ Teaspoon Salt

Directions:

1. Add cream cheese, sugar substitute, salt and vanilla extract to a blender. Blend it until smooth.
2. Slowly add the heavy cream.
3. Continue to blend until it's thickened, which will take one to two minutes. It should have a mousse like consistency once you're done.
4. Spoon the mixture into a piping bag and pipe into 8 mini cupcake liners. Chill for one hour until they are set. Keep them refrigerated.

Nutrition Facts per Serving:

- Total Carbs: 1.05 grams
- Dietary Fiber: 0 grams
- Net Carbs: 1.05 grams
- Protein: 1.66 grams
- Total Fat: 8.86 grams
- Calories: 91

MATCHA LATTE LIQUID FAT BOMB

Matcha is a green tea that has a very strong, potent flavor. This liquid fat bomb is a little different from the solid fat bombs, but it will provide you with the healthy fat you need for the Ketogenic diet. Remember it does only make one serving at a time, but it means that it tastes fresh!

- Prep Time: 5 Minutes
- Total Time: 10-15 Minutes

- Serves: 1
- Dairy Free, Nut Free

Ingredients:

- ½ Cup Boiling Water
- 1 Teaspoon Matcha Powder
- ⅓ Cup Unsweetened Coconut Milk
- 1 Tablespoon MCT Oil (you can also use extra virgin coconut oil)
- 3 Drops Liquid Stevia

Directions:

1. Start by mixing the matcha powder in the boiling water. Make sure it's completely combined.
2. Add MTC oil and whisk it all over again.
3. Use a milk frother to make the coconut milk froth. Next, pour the froth into the glass with your matcha, and sprinkle matcha powder on top.
4. Add the sweetener before serving. (Optional)

Nutrition Facts per Serving:

- Total Carbs: 6.29 grams
- Dietary Fiber: 2.1 grams
- Net Carbs: 4.09 grams
- Protein: 1.8 grams
- Total Fat: 32.5 grams
- Calories: 311

CHOCOLATE MOUSSE

Chocolate mousse is known to be simplistic but very satisfying. This is one way to take care of your sweet tooth, especially if you're having a chocolate craving. It's easy, dairy free, and it's packed with the good fats that you need.

- Prep Time: 5 Minutes
- Total Time: 10-15 Minutes
- Serves: 2

- Dairy Free

Ingredients:

- 1 Cup Creamed Coconut Milk
- 3 Tablespoons Raw Cocoa Powder
- 6-12 Drops Liquid Sweetener
- Fresh Cream and Dark Chocolate for Topping (Optional)

Directions:

1. Mix coconut milk, raw cocoa powder and liquid sweetener with a mixer. Remember that your mousse needs to be really smooth, so you need to keep mixing it until it has a smooth consistency.
2. Top with the fresh cream and dark chocolate.

Nutrition Facts per Serving

- Total Carbs: 11.37 grams
- Dietary Fiber: 5.1 grams
- Net Carbs: 6.27 grams
- Protein: 4.21 grams
- Total Fat: 29.67 grams
- Calories: 294

PEANUT BUTTER BALLS

Peanut butter is extremely high in fat, so you'll be able to use it in most keto recipes. You can keep these delightful peanut butter balls in the fridge or at room temperature.

- Prep Time: 5 Minutes
- Cook Time: 1 Hour
- Serves: 8
- Dairy Free

Ingredients:

- ¼ Cup Peanut Butter
- 2 Tablespoons Butter
- 1 Tablespoon Coconut Oil
- ¼ Cup Peanuts, Crushed
- 3 Drops Liquid Sweetener

Directions:

1. Melt butter, coconut oil and peanut butter in a saucepan over low heat, stirring until combined.
2. Add in your sweetener, and continue to stir.
3. Place the mixture into the freezer for 10 minutes.
4. Form mixture into balls, and then roll them in crushed peanuts.
5. Let chill for at least one hour before serving.

Nutrition Facts per Serving

- Total Carbs: 2.66 grams
- Dietary Fiber: 1 grams
- Net Carbs: 1.66 grams
- Protein: 3.18 gram
- Total Fat: 9.95 grams
- Calories: 107

PERFECTLY PINK BOMBS

These fat bombs are pretty and pink, and they're a perfect addition to your keto diet! Remember that fresh fruit is always best, but frozen fruits can be used, too.

- Prep Time: 5 Minutes
- Total Time: 10-15 Minutes
- Serves: 6
- Nut Free

Ingredients:

- 4 Tablespoons Coconut Oil
- 4 Cherries, Pitted
- 4 Strawberries, Diced
- 2 Ounces Half & Half
- Liquid Sweetener to Taste

Directions:

1. Place your cherries and strawberries in a blender and blend until completely pureed.
2. Add in your half & half, and then add in your liquid sweetener. Blend until completely mixed together.
3. Melt your coconut oil and blend it in.
4. Pour in molds and let freeze. Keep refrigerated.

Nutrition Facts per Serving:

- Total Carbs: 1.93 grams
- Dietary Fiber: 0.3 grams
- Net Carbs: 1.63 grams
- Protein: 0.41 grams
- Total Fat: 10.19 grams
- Calories: 97

TWO-INGREDIENT CRANBERRY FAT BOMBS

These cranberry bombs are just sweet enough to curb your sweet tooth and your appetite, but they have a tang to them that anyone is sure to love.

- Prep Time: 5 Minutes
- Total Time: 15-20 Minutes
- Serves: 6
- Nut Free, Sweetener Free

Ingredients:

- 2/3 Cup Cranberries, Dried
- 6 Ounces mascarpone Cheese, Softened

Directions:

1. Chop your cranberries. Make sure that they're chopped fine.
2. Soften your mascarpone cheese, and then blend all ingredients together.
3. Gently spoon the mixture into mini muffin liners and chill for about an hour in the refrigerator before serving.

Nutrition Facts per Serving

- Total Carbs: 3 grams
- Dietary Fiber: 1 gram
- Net Carbs: 2 grams
- Protein: 7 grams
- Total Fat: 10 grams
- Calories: 125

CHAPTER 4

15 SAVORY FAT BOMBS

If you're not only looking for a fat bomb that is sweet, then you'll want to check out these simple but savory fat bomb recipes. These fat bombs are easy to make. Many of them can be made with multiple servings in under 15 minutes.

SALMON FAT BOMBS

Salmon is high in healthy fats, making it perfect for this fat bomb recipe. You can also substitute for mackerel instead if you want a different taste.

- Prep Time: 5 Minutes
- Total Time: 10-15 Minutes
- Serves: 6
- Nut Free, Sweetener Free

Ingredients:

- ½ Cup Full-Fat Cream Cheese
- 5 Tablespoons Butter
- 1.8 Ounces Smoked Salmon
- 1 Tablespoon Lemon Juice
- 1 ½ Tablespoons Fresh Dill, Chopped

Directions:

1. Start by putting your cream cheese, butter and smoked salmon into a food processor.
2. Add in your dill and lemon juice, pulsing until smooth.
3. Take a tray lined with parchment paper, and then use about 2 ½ tablespoons of the mixture to form each piece. Add more dill for garnish, and allow to firm in the fridge for one to two hours.

Nutrition Facts per Serving

- Total Carbs: 0.8 grams
- Dietary Fiber: 0.1 grams
- Net Carbs: 0.7 grams
- Proteins: 3.2 grams
- Total Fat: 15.7 grams
- Calories: 147

CHEESE & TOMATO BITES

If you like something that has the taste of summer, then this is the recipe for you. If you don't have fresh chives, dried chives will work as well. You can also add oregano, thyme, basil or even rosemary in this recipe.

- Prep Time: 5-10 Minutes
- Cook Time: 15-20 Minutes
- Serves: 12
- Sweetener Free

Ingredients:

- 3 Ounces Full Fat Cream Cheese
- 12 Cherry Tomatoes
- ¼ Cup Fresh Chives
- Salt to Taste

Directions:

1. Cut a small slice off the top of each cherry tomato and discard seeds and juice.
2. Chop your chives thin, and then mix it with your softened cream cheese and salt.
3. Fill each tomato with flavored cream cheese.

Nutrition Facts per Serving

- Total Carbs: 1.03 grams
- Dietary Fiber: 0.2 grams
- Net Carbs: 0.83 grams
- Protein: 0.83 grams
- Total Fat: 2.74 grams
- Calories: 31

BACON & GREEN ONIONS

This is a bold choice, especially if you're a bacon lover. The green onions and bacon complement each other well from crisp to greasy, and they're best to serve warm.

- Prep Time: 5 Minutes
- Total Time: 15 Minutes
- Serves: 5
- Nut Free, Dairy Free, Sweetener Free

Ingredients:

- 5 Strips Bacon
- 6 Green Onions, Trimmed
- 4 Tablespoons Coconut Oil
- Salt and Pepper to Taste

Directions:

1. Start by wrapping green onions together using a single strip of bacon. Repeat until all of your bacon and green onions are used.
2. Season the wrapped green onions with salt and pepper.
3. Use a frying skillet and heat up coconut oil over medium high heat, frying your wraps until they're slightly browned. This usually takes six to eight minutes.

Nutrition Facts per Serving:

- Total Carbs: 2.82 grams
- Dietary Fiber: 0.8 grams
- Net Carbs: 2.02 grams
- Protein: 1 gram
- Total Fat: 12.5 grams
- Calories: 121

CRUNCHY AVOCADO BOMBS

Avocados are full of healthy fats, which work perfectly for this recipe. You'll find that with a dash of pecan, it has just enough flavor to make it mouthwatering.

The best part of this recipe is that with three ingredients, it's incredibly simple, and it has a texture that you're sure to love.

- Prep Time: 5 Minutes

- Total Time: 15 Minutes
- Serves: 8
- Dairy Free, Sweetener Free

Ingredients:

- 6 Pecans
- 2 Avocados
- 4 Slices Bacon

Directions:

1. Cook your bacon in a pan over medium-high heat until the bacon is crispy.
2. Take it off of heat, allowing it to cool before crumbling it.
3. Take a bowl and mash your avocados, and then crumble your pecans.
4. Mix all ingredients together, and make round balls using an ice cream scooper.

Nutrition Facts per Serving

- Total Carbs: 4.74 grams
- Dietary Fiber: 3.6 grams
- Net Carbs: 1.14 grams
- Protein: 2.86 grams
- Total Fat: 14.27 grams
- Calories: 151

KETO PARMESAN PESTO DIP

This dip is great to serve with crisp lettuce or cucumber sticks. You can also try it with kale if you want a crisp, bitter crunch. It tastes better cold, but it can be served at room temperature as well.

- Prep Time: 5 Minutes
- Total Time: 5 Minutes
- Serves: 6 (about two tablespoons)

- Nut Free, Sweetener Free

Ingredients:

- 1 Cup Full Fat Cream Cheese
- 2 Tablespoons Basil Pesto
- ½ Cup Parmesan Cheese, Grated
- 8 Olives, Sliced
- Salt and Pepper to Taste

Directions:

1. Mix all of your ingredients together in a mixing bowl.
2. Refrigerate for at least 20 minutes before serving.

Nutrition Facts per Serving:

- Total Carbs: 3.43 grams
- Dietary Fiber: 0.2 grams
- Net Carbs: 3.23 grams
- Protein: 5.42 grams
- Total Fat: 14.33 grams
- Calories: 161

BACON & PECAN ROLLS

This recipe is quick and easy to make and enjoy. If you want to add a little more spice, then basil is a great addition to this recipe. Onion powder can also give it extra flavor. Try and see what works best for you!

- Prep Time: 5 Minutes
- Total Time: 15 Minutes
- Serves: 12
- Sweetener Free

Ingredients:

- 4 Bacon Slices, Cooked
- ½ Cup Pecan Halves, Chopped
- ½ Cup Organic Butter
- 1 Teaspoon Garlic Powder

Directions:

1. Divide your bacon into three parts, and then spread each part with butter.
2. Press your pecan pieces into the butter.
3. Sprinkle with garlic and roll up.

Nutrition Facts per Serving

- Total Carbs: 0.83 grams
- Dietary Fiber: 0.4 grams
- Net Carbs: 0.43 grams
- Protein: 1.53 grams
- Total Fat: 14.87 grams
- Calories: 139

SOUR CREAM BACON DIP

With both cream cheese and sour cream, this dip is smooth and rich in flavor. It's a perfect fat bomb as well as a party dip.

- Prep Time: 5-10 Minutes
- Total Time: 40 Minutes
- Serves: 12
- Nut Free, Sweetener Free

Ingredients:

- 5 Slices Bacon, Cooked & Crumbled
- 1 ½ Cups Sour Cream
- 1 Cup Cream Cheese
- 1 Cup Cheddar Cheese, Shredded
- 1 Cup Scallions, Sliced

Directions:

1. Start by heating your oven to 400 degrees F (200 degrees C).
2. Combine all of your ingredients together in a bowl, and then spoon out onto a baking dish.
3. Cook for 25 to 35 minutes. The cheese should be bubbling when it's done.
4. Let it cool slightly before serving.

Nutrition Facts per Serving:

- Total Carbs: 3.5 grams
- Dietary Fiber: 0.2 grams
- Net Carbs: 3.3 grams
- Protein: 6.58 grams
- Total Fat: 16.76 grams
- Calories: 190

PIZZA SUPREME BOMB

If you love sausage pizza, then this is the fat bomb for you. It can certainly help you with your cravings during the Ketogenic diet.

- Prep Time: 5-10 Minutes
- Total Time: 15-25 Minutes
- Serves: 6
- Nut Free, Sweetener Free

Ingredients:

- 12 Italian Sausage Slices
- 8 Black Olives, Pitted
- ¾ Cup Cream Cheese
- 2 Tablespoons Basil, Fresh & Chopped
- 6 Cherry Tomatoes
- Salt to Taste

Directions:

1. Dice your olives and Italian sausage slices.
2. Mix tomatoes, basil and cream cheese together until thoroughly blended.
3. Add your sausage slices and olives into your cream cheese, and then mix thoroughly.
4. Form into balls, and garnish with more basil and olives if desired.

Nutrition Facts per Serving:

- Total Carbs: 1.92 grams
- Dietary Fiber: 0.3 grams
- Net Carbs: 1.63 grams
- Protein: 3.29 grams
- Total Fat: 11.26 grams
- Calories: 120

PARMESAN CHIPS

These Parmesan chips are a quick and easy snack, and you can always add extra herbs for a new twist. You can even try adding some cayenne to give them an extra kick!

- Prep Time: 5 Minutes
- Total Time: 15-20 Minutes
- Serves: 10
- Nut Free, Sweetener Free

Ingredients:

- 1 Cup Parmesan Cheese, Grated
- 4 Tablespoons Coconut Flour
- 1 Teaspoon Rosemary
- ½ Teaspoon Garlic Powder
- ½ Teaspoon Basil

Directions:

1. Start by heating your oven to 350 degrees F (180 degrees C), and then take your Parmesan and flour, mixing it together. Make sure that you use grated Parmesan cheese instead of powdery Parmesan cheese or it'll all start to fall apart.
2. Add your herbs and continue to mix everything together.
3. Line a large baking sheet with parchment paper. Spoon mixture 2 inches apart on prepared baking sheet.
4. Bake for 8-10 minutes or until crisp and golden.
5. Let cool and enjoy!

Nutrition Facts per Serving:

- Total Carbs: 1.76 grams
- Dietary Fiber: 0.1 grams
- Net Carbs: 1.66 grams
- Protein: 2.9 grams
- Total Fat: 2.8 grams
- Calories: 44

PORK & CASHEW SURPRISE

This is another quick and easy fat bomb recipe. The Dijon mustard gives it a great kick, but feel free to add salt, pepper and garlic to spice it up even more.

- Prep Time: 5-10 Minutes
- Total Time: 25 Minutes
- Serves: 12
- Sweetener Free

Ingredients:

- 3 Slices Pork Ham, Chopped
- 6 Ounces Sausage
- 6 Ounces Cream Cheese, Softened
- ¼ Cup Cashews, Chopped
- 1 Teaspoon Dijon Mustard

Directions:

1. Chop your sausages and pop them in the blender with your cashews, blending until smooth.
2. Beat the cream cheese and mustard together until smooth.
3. Roll your sausage mixture into balls and then form a cream cheese layer over it with your fingers. It should make about twelve balls.
4. Refrigerate them until firm, and then roll each ball in the chopped smoke pork ham before serving.

Nutrition Facts per Serving:

- Total Carbs: 3.63 grams
- Dietary Fiber: 0.2 gram
- Net Carbs: 3.43 grams
- Protein: 9.03 grams
- Total Fat: 12.33 grams
- Calories: 159

EGG & BLUE CHEESE FAT BOMBS

With cream cheese and blue cheese, you'll find that this fat bomb has a pungent taste. Feel free to add salt, pepper and even garlic to this fat bomb recipe.

- Prep Time: 5-10 Minutes
- Total Time: 15-20 Minutes
- Serves: 6
- Nut Free, Sweetener Free

Ingredients:

- 2 Eggs, Boiled and Chopped
- ¼ Cup Butter
- 1 Cup Cream Cheese
- ½ Cup Blue Cheese, Grated

Directions:

1. Mix cream cheese, grated blue cheese, and butter in a medium mixing bowl.
2. Add in eggs, and continue to stir, making sure it's mixed well.
3. Make six balls, and then place them on parchment paper. Refrigerate for about 2 hours.

Nutrition Facts per Serving:

- Total Carbs: 1.85 grams
- Dietary Fiber: 0 grams
- Net Carbs: 1.85 grams
- Protein: 7.65 grams
- Total Fat: 21.58 grams
- Calories: 231

THREE-INGREDIENT PESTO
BOMBS

This recipe only uses three ingredients and is surprisingly delicious. You can also use it as a dip and serve with your favorite vegetable sticks.

- Prep Time: 5 Minutes
- Total Time: 15 Minutes
- Serves: 4
- Nut Free, Sweetener Free

Ingredients:

- ½ Cup Cream Cheese
- ¼ Cup Pesto Sauce
- 6 Black Olives, Chopped

Directions:

1. Soften your cream cheese slightly, and then add the other two ingredients into the bowl, mixing completely.
2. Pour it into mini muffin cups, and then refrigerate.

Nutrition Facts per Serving:

- Total Carbs: 1.82 grams
- Dietary Fiber: 0.3 grams
- Net Carbs: 1.52 grams
- Protein: 3.68 grams
- Total Fat: 17.7 grams
- Calories: 177

EASY AVOCADO PROSCIUTTO FAT BOMBS

This fat bomb is made with only three ingredients, and you'll find it's simple to make without giving up its flavor due to that simplicity.

- Prep Time: 10 Minutes
- Total Time: 10 Minutes
- Serves: 10
- Nut Free, Sweetener Free, Dairy Free

Ingredients:

- 1 Avocado
- 1 Lime
- 10 Slices Prosciutto

Directions:

1. Halve your avocado, remove the seed, and then cut it into large slices.
2. Squeeze lime over avocado slices, and then lay each prosciutto slice on a plate.
3. Place each avocado slice on each prosciutto slice, squeeze a little bit more lime, and roll the prosciutto slice up.

Nutrition Facts per Serving:

- Total Carbs: 2.7 gram
- Dietary Fiber: 1.4 gram
- Net Carbs: 1.3 grams
- Protein: 2.9 grams
- Total Fat: 4.5 grams
- Calories: 60

GARLIC & LEMON FAT BOMBS

Easy to make and taste wonderful, these fat bombs will surprise you with its sour flavor and its creamy texture.

- Prep Time: 5 Minutes
- Total Time: 10 Minutes
- Serves: 12
- Nut Free, Sweetener Free

Ingredients:

- ¾ Cup Butter
- 4 Ounces Cream Cheese
- 1 ½ Lemon
- ¼ Cup Fresh Garlic, Minced

Directions:

1. Soften butter and cream cheese, and then blend them with the lemon juice and garlic. Continue to blend until thoroughly mixed and fluffy.
2. Make small balls using an ice cream scooper on a plate and refrigerate for at least 1 hour before serving.

Nutrition Facts per Serving:

- Total Carbs: 1.68 grams
- Dietary Fiber: 0.1 grams
- Net Carbs: 1.58 grams
- Protein: 1.33 grams
- Total Fat: 10.45 grams
- Calories: 105

BACON CHEESE STICKS

Sometimes the best way to keep things tasty is to keep them simple, and that's exactly what this fat bomb recipe strives to do. Feel free to change the type of cheese that you use. Using maple or apple-smoked bacon will give this keto bomb some extra flavor, and thick cut bacon is usually best.

- Prep Time: 5 Minutes

- Total Time: 15 Minutes
- Serves: 4
- Nut Free, Sweetener Free

Ingredients:

- 4 Slices Bacon
- 4 Frigo Strings of Cheese (Emmental cheese is a great addition)

Directions:

1. Preheat the oven to 350 degrees F (180 degrees C).
2. Wrap cheese sticks with bacon and secure it together with a toothpick.
3. Bake in the oven for 8-10 minutes.
4. Remove and place on a paper towel to drain while cooling.

Nutrition Facts per Serving:

- Total Carbs: 0.42 grams
- Dietary Fiber: 0 grams
- Net Carbs: 0.42 grams
- Protein: 6.86 grams
- Total Fat: 15.3 grams
- Calories: 167

CHAPTER 5

BONUS KETO ICE CREAM RECIPES

Ice cream isn't something that you have to give up if you're on the Ketogenic diet. All three of these recipes will at least give you a small bowl in a single serving to sit down and enjoy your favorite frozen treat.

NO CHURN & EASY VANILLA
ICE CREAM

If you don't have cream of tartar, you can use ¼ teaspoon of apple cider vinegar, and you can easily turn this dairy-free by using coconut milk, which will work just as well for this sweet and simple recipe.

- Prep Time: 5-10 Minutes
- Total Time: 25-30 Minutes
- Serves: 1
- Nut Free

Ingredients:

- 4 Large Eggs, Separated
- ¼ Teaspoon Cream of Tartar
- ½ Cup Powdered Sweetener
- 1 ¼ Cup Heavy Whipping Cream
- 1 Tablespoon Vanilla Extract

Directions:

1. Start by separating egg yolks from egg whites, and whisk the egg whites with cream of tartar and powdered sweetener. The egg whites will begin to thicken. They should start to form stiff peaks, and you'll need to keep whisking until they do.
2. Take another bowl, and start to whisk your cream. Soft peaks should start to form as the whisk is removed, but you'll need to be careful not to over whisk the cream.
3. In a third bowl, combine egg yolks with vanilla.
4. Now you can fold your whisked egg whites into your now whipped cream.
5. Add in your egg yolk mixture, and continue to gently fold with a spatula until thoroughly combined.
6. Place it in a pan, preferably a loaf pan, and put it in the freezer and let chill for about two hours.

Nutrition Facts per Serving

- Total Carbs: 2.3 grams
- Dietary Fiber: 0 grams
- Net Carbs: 2.3 grams
- Protein: 5.1 grams
- Total Fat: 22.2 grams
- Calories: 238

CREAMY STRAWBERRY
ICE CREAM

Strawberries are great when they're fresh, but you'll need to freeze them either way to make this lovely dessert so buying frozen strawberries will work in a pinch. Coconut oil will also work if you don't have MCT oil on hand.

- Prep Time: 5 Minutes
- Total Time: 10-15 Minutes
- Serves: 6
- Dairy Free, Nut Free

Ingredients:

- 2 Cups Strawberries, Quartered
- 1 Teaspoon Vanilla Extract
- 1 ¼ Cup Creamed Coconut Milk
- ¼ Cup MCT Oil
- ¼ Cup Powdered Sweetener

Directions:

1. Quarter strawberries if they haven't been quartered in advance, and they'll need to be frozen for four to six hours. You can even leave them in overnight.
2. Afterwards, you can blend them in a blender with your creamed coconut milk, MCT oil, vanilla extract and powdered sweetener.
3. Continue to blend until completely smooth, and then pour in a freezer safe container.
4. Let freeze.
5. Let it soften at room temperature for about five minutes before serving.

Nutrition Facts per Serving:

- Total Carbs: 5.7 grams
- Dietary Fiber: 1 grams
- Net Carbs: 4.7 grams
- Protein: 1.8 grams
- Total Fat: 25.8 grams
- Calories: 255

SIMPLE COCONUT ICE CREAM
WITH A "MAGIC SHELL"

Although this is a two-step recipe, you'll find that both parts are easy to make and have very few ingredients. The chocolate shell that you're making will need to be kept in the fridge. A little more vanilla can be added if you want a bit more potent flavor, and Himalayan sea salt can be used to give it an extra kick as well.

- Prep Time: 10 Minutes
- Total Time: 35-40 Minutes
- Serves: 8
- Dairy Free, Nut Free

Ingredients:

For the ice cream:

- 1 Cup Coconut Cream

- 2 ½ Cups Liquid Coconut Milk
- ½ Cup Powdered Sweetener (Sugar Substitute)
- 1 Cup Shredded Coconut, Unsweetened
- 1 Teaspoon Vanilla Extract
- ¼ Teaspoon Salt

For the Chocolate Magic Shell:

You can always use 85% dark chocolate instead of using cocoa powder. A serving is two tablespoons.

- ½ Cup Coconut Oil, Melted
- ½ Cup Cocoa Powder, Unsweetened
- ¼ Cup Powdered Sweetener (Sugar Substitute)

Directions:

1. Start by toasting your shredded coconut in the oven. It'll need to be at 350 degrees F (180 degrees C), and make sure it's spread out, toasting for about 5-8 minutes. It should be a light golden color, but you'll want to mix it while cooking at least once to keep it from burning.

2. Take your coconut milk and your coconut cream, spooning it into a saucepan and heating over medium heat. Once it's hot, remove it from heat, and add in your sweetener, mixing until it's completely dissolved.

3. Add in your vanilla extract, salt and toasted coconut. Make sure to mix well.

4. Pour it all into a food processor, pulsing until it reaches a nice smooth consistency.

5. Pour the mixture into your ice cream maker, blending for about thirty to sixty minutes. Scoop it out, and put it in a freezer safe container. If you don't have an ice cream maker, then just mix vigorously every thirty minutes until frozen after placing it in the freezer.

6. Now, let's move on to making the 'magic shell' recipe. Mix coconut oil, powdered sugar and cocoa powder together in a bowl. Make sure it's completely combined. That's it! It's really that simple.

7. When serving, you'll want two scoops of ice cream with two tablespoons of the melted chocolate.

Nutrition Facts per Serving:

- Total Carbs: 14.7 grams
- Dietary Fiber: 3.7 grams
- Net Carbs: 11 grams
- Protein: 4 grams
- Total Fat: 33.14 grams
- Calories: 345

AFTERWORD

Now you have everything that you need to make sweet or savory fat bombs. With nut butter at your disposal and all of the information you need to get the right ingredients, you can now make all fat bombs that you can enjoy on a Ketogenic diet or other low-carb diets.

Just remember to make sure all of your ingredients don't have hidden sugars, and take time to find the sugar substitute that's right for you, and you'll have everything that you need to make all these tasty fat bombs!

AUTHOR'S NOTE

Hi there! Thank you so much for taking the time to read my book. I hope you have enjoyed reading this book as much as I've enjoyed writing it. If you enjoyed this book, please consider leaving a review on Amazon. Your support really means a lot and keeps me going.

If you have any questions, please don't hesitate to contact me at ask@cleaneatingspirit.com

Don't forget to follow me on Facebook and Instagram for more information related to health and wellness.

Facebook: https://www.facebook.com/cleaneatingspirit

Instagram: https://www.instagram.com/cleaneatingspirit

Made in the USA
San Bernardino, CA
25 February 2019